Autumn Lamp in Rain

Poetry by

Han Glassman

Autumn Lamp in Rain

Poetry by

Han Glassman

The Oliver Arts & Open Press

Library of Congress Control Number: 2011929522
Glassman, Han (Yoo Han Pil). 1930-
Autumn Lamp in Rain
Poetry by Han Glassman

ISBN: 978-0-9829878-1-0

"Ash Wednesday" appeared in The 100th Street News: A Monumental Block
"Swan Lake" appeared in Nomad's Choir and in the 100th Street Newsletter
"Spring Abandoned" appeared in Smoke Signals under the pen-name Han Misyou
"Foreign Night," "Barrier to Spring" and "Autumn Illumination" appeared in Nomad's Choir under the pen-name Han Misyou
"Thomas," "Brown Leaves" and "The Colony" appeared in The New Press under the pen-name Han Misyou
"Autumn Love," "Defense," "Your Image," "Retrieve," "Distant Spring," "Holidays," "Brotherhood" and "Autumn Lamp" appeared in The National Library of Poetry under the pen-name Han Misyou

The Oliver Arts & Open Press
2578 Broadway (Suite #102)
New York, NY 10025
http://oliveropenpress.com

For My Family

CONTENTS

Autumn Lamp in Rain

Prologue

The Japanese occupied Korea, the country I was born in, from 1910-1945. This harsh, brutal occupation was the most influential experience of my childhood, and it infuses every aspect of my poetry. Every Korean family lost a loved one, and many lost several.

By the year 1940, with Japan well into the war effort, the occupying Japanese forces deployed our students and workforce into the war front. Most of these people never came home—their whereabouts have not been revealed to their families even to this day.

I lost my two sisters. They were just a little older than I. As a child, I would follow them wherever they went—chasing butterflies in summer, fireflies on winter evenings. I couldn't understand that they were gone, and I wouldn't accept the thought of losing them forever. I would run under the trees, calling out their names, thinking my voice would make them appear. Their absence was everywhere. The hollowness dug into me. It was as if my shoulders had been removed from my body. This is the meaning of family. Each member is an organ for the larger whole.

What happened to my family, to my country, is unjust. The American sailors at Pearl Harbor should have had their chance to live out their lives, not be left to lie at the bottom of the sea. That too was unjust. My sisters and all the other Korean youths who never returned home should have come home by now. That would have been just. The September 11 workers at the World Trade Center should have had dinner that night together with their families. That would have been just.

God grant mercy on the bereaved. In spasms of despair, they have no one to turn to, like people with neither home nor food. They roam the streets knocking at the house of a stranger for help. When I was young and such a person came to our house, my mother used to say, "Let's skip our dinner and give it to him." I pick up my blue pen and try to go on writing my poetry. Even with sleepless nights and powerless words, I must write. The story of those who suffered must be told. It's the only way to lend justice to the bereaved, to feed a despairing heart, however long ago the wounds were inflicted.

•

This book is made possible by the contribution of my family. My husband, Frederic, is a Holocaust survivor from Romania. As a man of culture he encourages me to write poems by introducing me to great works of humanism in the European arts, literature and music. His help is not only in his encouragement, but we actually write our poetry together.

Like many other immigrants in America, he slept fewer hours to raise a family. Our first daughter, Diana, is a Harvard graduate with an MBA and MPA (Public Administration), and the other, Grace, is a medical doctor.

Even with their busy hours, my daughters always took time to review my English grammar. Whenever possible, on sunny Sunday afternoons, my daughters' husbands, Evan and Joseph, joined us in Riverside Park in New York City. These young men would run with our family dog far to the banks of the Hudson, giving us a sense of solidarity.

Family means home, work and peace. The rest is not in our hands. We cautiously hold each other trying to cross a reed bridge.

September 9, 2007

Han Glassman and
co-author Frederic,
my husband.

To My Sisters

For sixty years I have waited for you.
My business with the world is over,
Suicidal ashes.

I close the old house that
you and I once shared
on this green earth.

One step closer to generous heaven
I climb up the high mountain
where Christ fell and cried.

> "Do you hear me?
> Do you see me?"

Preface to "Dream"

August 15, 1945: the day of Japan's surrender to the Allies. Celebration, freedom and joy for the liberated people in Asia, of course. But beneath the flow of joy, what human cost! The number of deaths during the withdrawal of the Japanese forces from the occupied nations was great and yet went largely undocumented.

In the late stage of the Pacific war my two sisters were in Shinkyo, Manchuria, forced there to serve the Empire. Malnourished and cold, one of them caught tuberculosis during her forced service. My first sister, Chang Sook Yoo, came home and died in February, 1945. On August 13 of that year I received a long letter from my second sister in Manchuria, Kyung Sook Yoo. The words on the paper were blurred by my tears, thinking about our dead sister, Chang Sook.

Meanwhile, Kyung Sook's life in Manchuria was in jeopardy. The surrender hastened the Japanese troops' desperate speed, leaving behind not only Korean workers but also their own Japanese civilians. The resentful Chinese, who themselves suffered under the brutal hand of the Japanese, began to retaliate indiscriminately against anyone they thought was Japanese. The Koreans, who couldn't speak Chinese, weren't able to explain they were not Japanese.

With the Japanese retreating, the Red Army invaded Manchuria and advanced down to the 38th parallel in Korea. Violence, rape, pillaging and the taking of human life were rampant. The people, the very streets, were frozen with fear. Where is my sister! Where is my sister! I did not know that that letter from Kyung Sook was the last I would receive from her on this earth. Ever since that year, 1945, a faithful memory has walked with me. Tonight the memory takes me into a sad dream.

Dream

Strange!
The town is as ancient as our Old Kingdom.
Nothing is changed.
I am with my sisters as before the Pacific War.
Hand in hand we all three walk around the town.
Our neighbors sit on a summer night, sharing
Small talk with each other. As before, our house
stands on the leafy roadside.
"It is late. More than 60 years have passed.
Let's go home. They are waiting, our parents."

September 27, 2007

A Small Shrine and A Poet

In the corner of the room;
A small shrine,
Candle-lights,
Blue incense.

Their sacred offerings remove the distance
Between departed ones and me.
Past love gradually walks into the room,
Warming the cold of life.

Our small talks are shared in the kitchen
And near the family hearth.
The winter night stays with us in a soft blanket.
The poet with the romantic nature wants to continue

Living here if possible.
A thunder storm hits the town.
Rent is overdue.
He may lose the room!

So be it.
The home of art
Is not steady anyway.
He turns the light on

And sits before the dark.
What to write...
when values are
In bank notes or money markets.

What to write...
When machines take over human feeling?
What can he do?
Let things be as they are.

He just keeps writing, honoring
love and small talk in the room
and respecting the woods and the river.

November 28, 2008

Miracle on the Snowy Lane

Sparkling in the evening lights,
Snow falls.
I walk on the snowy lane in Riverside Park
People move past quietly.

In the fresh air I feel easy
and unchallenged to myself
Because I am free from pen and paper.
Myself unaware,
I follow the events of my former years —

After a long day's labor, with friends
I would go to the tea room, a poet's habitat
Its wall lined with classic records
and old violins.

> Oh God, stop time here,
> give us repose.
> The resounding music is
> fading into the good night.

For us time did not stop there in the tea room.
Early next morning the Korean War broke out.
War business is so cheap that it can assault
any country on a penny invitation!

We ran away
from hunger and carnage
Only to chase
Hunger and carnage.

In this way when the memory walks with me,
Someone, behind me,
Gently taps my shoulder
Offering a lit cigarette.

Shall I accept it?
From a stranger!
No, he cannot be. I met him
Somewhere in that war-torn country.

In an auditorium of poetry reading, possibly.
The reading room was moist
with tears of love for the country.
It was a rainy day in October.

"It's you, my friend.
Grieving much on a mortal path
I have been looking for you
Ever since that October.

"Why... you alone, cold!
Shall I walk with you?"
His voice is nothing but humble sincerity.
"To where?" I barely ask.

On a winter night when snow falls in silence,
He and I walk together.

October 1989

Trees Echo

Sunrays pierce through the forest of oaks.
Along the forest a river flows with iridescent facets —
Swans are there, stars are there.

You touch, you love nature's things
with a desperate desire to stay here and write.
To stay here? Why... of course.

You are an alien, you must go somewhere.
But to where, to another Troy?
Obey the law or disobey...

Either way you have no choice but to live.
You ask the woody walls
"Are you here with me, Christ, are you?"

The trees echo.
"Of course, you are with Him.
We are part of Him, crucified together.

"Before Calvary Day
Not sipping even a drop of rain,
We decided to desiccate ourselves

"So that the burden of the Cross-Wood
On his shoulders
Might be less.

"Barriers to the Romans were what we should have been,
Protection against the pounding hammer on the nails.
Steel and iron shields are what we should have been.

"With anointed resin
Our nailed holes are healed now.
Our herbs cleanse human wounds

"Stay with us, don't go away."
Song birds stay with the trees.
You stay, too.

June 1987

Change

All changes.
High towers for high rent.
Small stores disappear.

All goes to the wireless journey of living.
Human voices become far. Poetry farther.
It is twilight, leaves are falling.

We too reached
the twilight
of our age.

Let's stop here and
exchange our anxieties
with friendship and love.

March 5, 2008

Lyrical House

Plunged into the pathos of war,
And into the ashes of migration later,
We lost each other and everything.
Pen and papers are all that I have now,
And your spirit between.

I know, by writing something,
I must bring you closer.
But my words are in chaos and disorder.
I put the pen and paper aside,
And follow your spirit.

Under the starry skies we walk. It seems
Stars and trees are ready to join us
We feel the joy of existence.

To enjoy the night perfectly
We secure our bed
And have bread and wine
On the table.
But how?

Find a home in the book
We carry in our pocket. The book is real
And home is free in the book,
A summer home
with grasshoppers jumping.

Or a winter home
where we can chop wood
And cook under the fire.
We build a lyrical house
So that we can write.

July 23, 2009

Orpheus

For a long time
I haven't been able
To write a line of verse.
I step out into the wet darkness.
Chaos, madness all around.

The familiar road, the same trees,
The loyal little creatures are
My sole companions.
The future will only be emptier
For I have not written even a single line of poetry.

To my right
cars press the road
and press each other.
The nose of one nudges
Irritably against the tail
Of another.

On my left
A long stone wall broods in icy air.
Leaning against the wall a man is squatting.
A lyre sits beside him —
Possibly a shadow of Eurydice.

Before he came to this city
He wanted to rescue his wife from hell,
And come together with her here. They would make
A feast of art, of literature.
And of music they love.

Defying Hades
He turned his head to see whether
His wife was following him.
Then she was no more!
Love turned to smoky ashes.

Only through
The pitiful tones of the lyre
Can he return to the past.

Talking to her about the snow storm
and sleepless nights without her:
About poetry and books
In the sunset window,
the lyrical pages
written by him and Eurydice
In the winter kitchen.

Windy, windy. It is January,
Dark and melancholy.
Full with warmth and love
Pigeons, squirrels come close to him.
Who is he?

People call him homeless.
For us he is our breadman, walnut man
And a musician who builds
A house of god's lyre every year
In the summer valleys.

He is our beloved Orpheus
Drifting from city to city.
The more dark and melancholy
The more urgent is
The call of his lyre.

With his little creatures
And herb-strung melodies
He threads together
The business of poverty
And loneliness.

January 1988

Leaving the City on the Blizzard Night

Thick fog-filled air is studded
with snowflakes and snow trees
like royal brocade
drawn from heaven.

Wherever you go, you cannot be seen.
The terrible world vanished.
You are safe now, you an alien,
a drifting poet in the third language

An unremitting fugitive without a crime.
Watchful eyes are no more.
Unleash and let him run free,
Apollo your dog, your sole companion.

I have lost everything
in this foreign land.
Deportation is imminent.
A drunken devil cries in my head.

The evening city
has many colored lamps
in the snow distance.
The red-green traffic lights

and cozy yellow lanterns
along the park lanes are
abandoned gypsy jewelry,
signs of an illusory destination.

You leave the fabulous city
with empty hands
believing that the downy snow silk
will gently house both of you.

Don't fall asleep
you and Apollo.
Spring will come. Snow
will melt. You will live.

A Facet of Poetry in Asia

Stars of Asian nights.
Acacia flowers.
The trill of the nightingale.
Crickets sing as they did a thousand years ago.

The lyric of the old kingdom
Is written on the soil
That trees grow from
With love and trust.

Mother's Day

Tanks, missiles, machine guns,
Rain of bombs from the sky.
At the center of the war, unable to move,
A wounded mother sits still
With her child on her knees.

Who has the power to raise
A family above time and place?

Her enormous pain.
She wants to continue holding the child
One minute more, two or three...

May 11, 2008
Mother's Day

Out of Print

Fear, uncertainty, family loss.
But we have lived somehow.
That is good enough.

So an exiled judge says.
He is aging. His voice sounds humane,
Reflecting the solitude of a winter night.
I agree, I have no defense.
Rain covers the evening, cold.

Hoping to find a friendly place
I wander into a small book store
The books I would like to have

Are out of print.
But somehow we eat and sleep.
That is good enough.

Golden Lights

Autumn night in exile.
Solitude and insomnia.
I sit on the door step.
The falling leaves cover the night.

Rooftops, cars and streetlights
Cast a golden silhouette
Against the evening sky,
Quiet and peaceful.

I hear the sound of
Lingering voices from afar—
But human presence is missing here.
The world seems like a far-off place.

The silence
Of the avenue-lamps
Tells you why the night is
So passionate and alone.

I follow the string of lamps.
At the gate of an Episcopal church
A cop bends over a homeless man
To see if he is alive.

I have grown old
Giving thanks
To the patrolman
And to the God of lights.

Literary Night

The intimacy of a literary night.
We shut the door against the storm.
The icy roads below the window
Sleep on our small talks – warm and affectionate.

Old dear friends are with us.
After the thankless job of lonely writing,
How sweet it is
When we are together.

There are icy wine glasses
On the table — we are relaxing
As we yearn for beauty,
Nature and God

In order to prolong
This blessed moment
We are busy packing the memories
With pink ribbons.

Romantic Artists

A window with lamps inside.
The old typewriter is still working.
A tavern violin, hanging on the wall

Is ready to play for
the safe return of the gypsy
from the snow storm.

One would like to go in behind the window
and relax in the beauty of an old place,
waiting to hear the violin

play again for the
return of the gypsy
from darkness and snow.

To the Reader:
My husband of close to 50 years and my partner in my poetry suddenly
passed away on February 15, 2009. We had just finished eating breakfast
together that day.

> *Dear Fred,*
> *This is the last poem from my collection. It was written at night,*
> *and the next day you and I were supposed to review it as we did all*
> *the other poems. Then, suddenly, you left. I hope you can hear*
> *me reading it now.*
>
> *Han*

Ash Wednesday

Grey February is atoning.
Clad in snow-patches here and there
the earth is fasting.

Following the grace of Ash Wednesday
thunder storms withdraw.
Ice melts, rocks seem softer.

Recalling the pain of Christ
even nature seems to pray for
God's absolution.

At last God grants us spring,
In a quiet recess along the river
Budding lilacs dream a genesis dream.

A dream as fresh as the hand of spring.
As tender as the white handkerchief
which would cleanse the tears of Christ's blood.

Sleep well, Fred, until I join you soon.

February 15, 2009
Fred's final day

In Remembrance of Our Father
Eulogy from Fred's Memorial Service

Thank you for joining our family in remembering my father today. I believe he is with us today, and will be always. I want him to hear how much his family loved him, what a wonderful husband and father he was, and how many lives he touched. And I'd like to share with you, our closest friends and family, a few stories about his life that you may not know—because he was quiet and humble and didn't talk about himself unless asked.

Life was initially not kind to my father. He was born in Bucharest, Romania, in 1926. As a boy, probably just when he was beginning to form his view of the world and people, Jews began to be persecuted in Europe. He encountered hatred, discrimination, betrayal and the worst examples of human behavior. And that time in his life, which should have been filled with happiness, was filled with fear instead. Not the kind of small worries that children encounter while growing up, but real fear, like whether you would get deported to a concentration camp at a moment's notice or be shot in the street. And he lived with those terrors for many, many years.

He was expelled from schools and put into forced labor for the Nazis. Everything was taken away from him. By some miracle, he and his parents survived. After the war, the Soviets occupied Romania, and at that time life was every bit as hard for the Jews as it had been under the Nazis. My father's dream was to become a doctor, but he was expelled from medical school. He finally escaped from Romania and settled in the United States when he was in his thirties. He tried to get into medical school here, but there were quotas on Jews in this country, too.

He came here with nothing in his pockets and started over from scratch. He met his wife, Han, who had survived the Japanese occupation of Korea, the Second Word War, and the Korean War. He fell in love with her and married her, and they had two children. He managed to get his parents out of Romania, and they joined him here. To support everyone, he worked two jobs at the same time. He concentrated on his new family in America and put behind him the pain from Europe.

His family was everything to him. He truly was a splendid father, a devoted husband, and a caring son. He would have done anything for us. We had very little money growing up—for years we didn't even have a telephone—but he made sure that my sister and I had a full and rich childhood. In his free time, he took us around the city, finding inexpensive ways to entertain us. We would ride the Staten Island Ferry just to see the beautiful view. He would take us to the old FAO Schwartz and let us spend hours there playing with the toys. He passed the time quietly, watching over us and enjoying the model train displays, which he loved. He took us to Coney Island, the Central Park Zoo, Chinatown, and Riverside Park. We loved our outings, and we loved him.

My mother, with whom he was married for almost 50 years, shared some beautiful stories with me. She said that we truly meant everything to him. When we were babies in the crib, he would come home from work every night, remove his beret and bow to us, lovingly. At Christmastime, he would buy an enormous bag of toys and hide them from us in the kitchen. He would stay up all night creating an elaborate alpine village with lights and an electric train set under the tree. To this day, he kept most of those toys to remember us by.

In all my memories of him, he never spent anything on himself. What little he had, it was all for us. Or sometimes it was for someone who had even less, like a homeless person. This is the kind of selfless man that he was.

He received some money from a Holocaust victims' fund, but he would not touch it because he wanted to leave it for Diana and me. He played the lottery everyday, hoping to win something big—not for himself, but for his children. Even as his health was deteriorating, he often refused to buy the things that would make his life a little easier, like a more comfortable pair of shoes for his painful legs or a new bed. It made him happier, I came to realize, to feel like he was doing something good for his family.

He would help my mother in every way possible. She writes poetry, but her English is not perfect. He would patiently edit her writing and encourage her unfailingly in her passion. He fixed things around the house for her, including her old manual typewriter that was always breaking down. He always tried to make her comfortable. Even when his health was failing, he got up on a ladder and managed to open the impossibly tough-to-open windows because she couldn't sleep with the them closed.

You would think, considering the background he came from, that he might have ended up bitter and hard. But he did not. He was always calm, gentle, generous, and wise. He was kind, witty, thoughtful, gracious, and positive. He was a good listener. Every person he met seemed to be inspired or moved by him. Many friends have said how he reminded them of a beloved departed grandfather or father. He was forgiving. If we had an argument, I could call him an hour later and it was as though it never happened; the things that had been said were already forgotten. He had seen too much in life to worry over the little things.

As adults, my sister and I spent a lot of time trying to make his life more comfortable and trying to make him happier. But, in retrospect, I think that he was happy. He had all the things he wanted around him—he had his family and he had his dog, Bogey, whom he adored and cared for like a child. He would take long walks everyday with him in Riverside Park and on Broadway, and he loved those walks. Every dog-owner in the neighborhood knew him as the kind old man with the lovely European accent who would hand out treats and knew each dog by name. His love for animals was unsurpassed. It was a reflection of the gentleness and beauty of his soul.

He was glad that Diana and I both married good men with kind families. And they became an extension of his family. He loved Evan and Joe like sons, and he loved their families too.

He was overjoyed with the birth of my son, Benjamin, 10 weeks ago. And he was so looking forward to the birth of Diana's baby. Benjamin was named after my father's father, which pleased him. He would call him "Boyum," the Romanian diminutive of Benjamin. I look at my son, and I know my father lives on in him—Benjamin resembles him and has his sunny, easy disposition. It breaks my heart to think that we will never hear him called Boyum again.

My father lives on in all of us. He was a truly special person. He showed us by example how to lead a beautiful life. He will be in our hearts and minds forever.

I love you, Daddy. We all love you.

Grace Glassman
For Frederic Glassman
February 25, 2009

Remembering Frederic Glassman

From *The 100th Street News: A Monumental Block*

The Block Association extends deepest sympathies to the family of Mr. Frederic Glassman, a resident of this block for almost 50 years, who departed this life in February. He was a devoted and loving husband, father and grandfather, and a kind, generous, gentle and wise man. He loved raising his children here and walking his dogs every day, first Apollo, then Bogey.

Mr. Glassman, a survivor of the Holocaust and of the Communist persecution of Jews in Romania, found peace and happiness in this country. His many friends on the block and in the neighborhood will miss him. He quietly inspired many and was admired by all who knew him.

He leaves behind his wife, Han, his daughters Diana and Grace, his sons-in-law Joe and Evan, his grandson Benjamin, and another grandchild on the way, and his dog Bogey. We miss him dearly.

Swan Lake

Snowy night, swan's melodies, attic windows look to
The lake. There in the window a poet sighs
An aching pain of the final hour.
The room is bare.
He has no reprieve back to the past;
The green bench was there by the lake,
Odette was dancing, swans were flowing melodiously.
Through the bridge of someone's violin
The swan's melody continues.
Dying, he comes close to the melody
That touches the chord of Nature.
Art is a steady bridge that enters soil, woods,
Water—painless, immutable.
To sustain Art's Bridge, one must grasp
Woodland chords, or the somersaulting cadence of
A swan in blue water.
Living on musical lyrics to honor Nature,
It takes more than genius.
Art died long ago at the market.
The myth of beauty, the treasure of the Universe
Is laid open, dissected, sterilized.
Native intimacy – art's call – escapes from
Woods, water, from the theaters, the academies.
The poet can hardly lift his pen,
He dies young on the anvil of adversity.
From the lake the indelible cadence of the swan
Echoes a tone of farewell to the window.
The sailing swan dripping starry tears
Glides into the woods.
Never say goodbye, never.
I was a fairy when I first met him by the lake,
As a fairy I will see the poet again.
In the woods, fairies dance high in the air.
As the wind reigns, snow falls,
Their tiny shoes shower over the lake.
In fleeting silk the fairy Queen floats
Into his room through the open window.
"It's me, the fairy.
Do you remember? Do you hear me?"
"Is it you...Odette...the swan...the lake...?"

He can barely breathe.
Something is unsaid, has been unsaid
In the years of privation,
In the years of the sick room.
It should be so, his poems are written
In the art of silence, on the bridge of the violin,
On the soil, in the woods.
When the aching pain of the final hour ends
The poet inherits a steady bridge to Nature —
There by the lake
The poet of the woods,
The fairy of the sailing swans.
Snowy night,
Swan's melodies
Love-granted night.

        Han and Frederic Glassman

Spring Abandoned

Fleeting people.
Fleeting cars.
Ages pass.
No words.
No love.
Spring stays with fallen angels
in an abandoned park.
Yet no matter how wretched they are
I can see in them a Native God.

Foreign Night

Sharp winds seek out people, blizzards sweep
All the way home. Black labor in black exile,
The day is over at last. You return to the room.

Twilight, fading oak twigs, unfinished verses
On the table. Below the dried twigs
You light a candle, burn incense.

How glad to have a gentle friend
With whom you can share a cup of tea, drawing
A small dialogue on life, art, snowy nights.

An illusion? Living by an illusion?
Yes, you must invent one. It is mercilessly clear
That life no longer has anything, not even a dream.

You sit by the candle, try to contemplate
The verses in the image of oak leaves
In the fall… pensive, violet-blue.

Words. Words are lonely here without seasons,
Songs, friends, not even a dream
On a snowy night.

You continue writing verses even if
There is no one to write for,
You continue burning a candle even if
There is no one to expect,

Because not to dream, not to love anything
Is impossible.

Barrier to Spring

Spring
Brilliantly defeated Spring
Spring, I have guarded your image
Like a memory of my homeland
And still guarding I must leave you
In the care of the terrible world.
The painter's brush, palette, canvas
I must put them aside
Oh Spring mild with bees, butterflies
Stay there
Stay there in the canvas!
The world is terrible
Oh the world's deadly pressure —
Barriers are absolute, orders are absolute
Obey the order
I have to kill or be killed by
Brother guerillas in the mountain
Where I played with them
A game of hide and seek years ago.

Autumn Illumination

It is Autumn.
Here by the law of seasons
All crises are canceled,
The space is safe.
Leaves flutter in the sun
Like golden butterflies,
Birds splash the fountain water.
Friends,
So long parted
By the war of NOT OUR WAR,
Let us be here together if possible
And saturate ourselves
In the small hour of ecstasy.
Friends, absent friends,
I have given you all my years
Among strangers in a strange land.
Separation,
The triumph of void.
Sad compromise shaped
Our lives too long.
It is late.
Foggy lamps, leafy benches and roads
Ethereally speak of mysteries—
Whenever you wish, my friends,
They can tell you
A tale of fairy nights,
Whenever you wish, they can illuminate
The stars,
So we may linger a little more.
It is so sweet for us
When we are together.

Thomas

All is analyzed, investigated
Thoroughly in this land
The future is blueprinted

In the blue and white paper
Is there any memory of the Earth?
Are there any tender words?

Is there any gentle stranger
With whom you might touch the snow
                jewels
Under the evening lamp?

Do not ask such lyrical questions —
Passions, free dreams are humiliated,
Thrown into the beggarly sky of a
                Painting
Hanging in a hallway

At the end of the hallway
Begin rooms number One Two — many
                more
Thomas — Second to The Last
Diana — The Last

It's amazing to see the weeping birds,
The weeping flowers in the picture
                frame
In this soul-less hallway

Young Thomas, the artist
Too tall to be with them in the frame
All day long

And wracked by doubt
Too small to perfect his images
He needs to change his mood

He appears at the Stray Tavern
When the chairs are stacked up
And the door is closed

He appears in the Spring mist
To see if the frame disappears
And the birds are free.

He knows
The blue-lined future is horizontal,
No vertical way of knowing the Soul...

> That can leap into the blue sky
> With unexpected joy
> When you see an old friend
> In a caged life of a hundred years

> God gave us a Soul as wings,
> The light and good Soul
> Which tries to draw us out of
> The labor cage, hard labor death

> No, It is not needed
> Spring is not needed

... And there is no way of attaining
Winged joy, free dreams
To ease the pain of living

Thomas knows
Horizontal days,
His years are programmed
For a hundred years of sleepless labor...

> But why such labor
> As long and old as empire?
> Is there any enemy left on the earth?

> Where is life?
> In the market!
> In the mercurial index up and down!

... And there is nothing new
On the flat horizon.

Brown Leaves

The gala of the summer leaves
Is over.

Now is the season
For you to go
For me to go too.

What can I say to you,
Dreamy foliage
Tinged with crushed jewels?

> That love wanted to linger
> In your bower...

> That beauty suffers injustice
> Short-shrifted ephemeral?

Choking back
Good-bye
To the sad tryst

You calmly accept brown crepe
And go with the wind.

The Colony

Empire's Dream
1910-1945

Snowy days stormy nights
Boots boots thunder
Boots boots sparkle

Vanguard soldiers thunder
Empire dreams sparkle
They take the whole world

Who can deal them a mighty blow?
Museums Archives — our treasure —
Are they safe, well hidden?

Forbidden is the Mother Tongue
By the bootman, the colonizer
It flees into passwords, and

Eyes relay messages signal by signal
Korea is underground. She is alone
No words from sons and daughters

Dragged into service of the Empire
Rice fields, pine trees, soaring cranes
Melodies of *Kayagum* strings

Ginseng harvests – no more
Forbidden are Korean names
Terrified Miss Lee is now

Second class Miss Toyota
Second class teacher among Japanese
Hey you Korean Mr. Suzuki

Too slow, action action, dig dig
Spade spade the earth for iron scraps
The iron for Fighters – *Kamikaze*

What is *Kamikaze*? God's Wind in the
              Pacific War: the Suicide —
              Against U.S. carriers
What is *Shinto*? Goddess's Way at the
              Shrine
Japanese *Shinto* like Santa

Korean kids believe it
"But why is there a shrine in your
              hand,
My child? Did you get it free?"

"No mother, I paid my Japanese
              teacher"
My mother screams
"Paid already! Such a high price for
              what?

For Goddess the *Amaterasu* way?
              For *Banzai* Japan?"
"No mother, the Goddess awaits in
              the shrine
For my prayer for our food and
              firewood the great grandma
              of the Emperor"

Korea is thoughtwashed, plundered,
              unarmed
Slaughtered. A cow cries "Get our
              country back!"
How? We will see

Fiery nights of Hiroshima
Red nights of Nagasaki
Boots boots stagger, boots boots
              tumble

The Empire falls, the Empire leaves
The toll was heavy. I lost my
        sisters –
Dragged to Manchuria in the service of
              the Empire

To find them
Over the 38th parallel of Yalta
Is the job of God

It happened in my early teens in that
Doomed August of 1945 when the
        world was
Colorful ticker tape dancing to
        the Allied victory

To hell with history! My mother
        passed away
I was left alone with my baby sister
Baby brother. The Korean war was
        pending

Yalta's Legacy
1945-1950

Is Korea truly liberated from Japan?
Ha ha ha... Yalta's Summit Trio
        laughs
Oh do not laugh Mr. Stalin Mr.
        Roosevelt

Mr. Churchill. Personally have you
        ever saved
One life, one tree with such
        awesome power?
Being a savior is harder than being a
        destroyer

The Earth and sky tremble
Universal history turns away
From the Earth. Do not laugh
What is in the cocktail glasses
At the Summit party?
White wine from Asian tears

From German tears
From European tears
To what future are the glasses
          toasted?

To the New Map of a double Korea,
Of a double Germany, of a double
          Europe
Do they know what they are
          drinking?

Shall we dare, shall we dare crack
Our heart and soul in two—like
North and South Korea? Can we? Can
          we?

Our business, impossible one, is to
          find
One grain of rice, two grains of rice
          for
The orphans, to house everyone
          before midnight

Korea, you are in God's hands now
Pray not to be another Troy
Pray not to be extinguished

Cold War Contest
1950-1953

Until the sunset hour we buried
Our mothers, fathers, colleagues and
Teachers – now but distant humanity.

Early Sunday morning June 1950
Yalta's 38th. Who can desecrate it?
The grasshoppers sing, and sing

"This is no man's zone
Leave us in peace, or we will pay
With all the lives of our Peninsula"
Sleeping trees by open windows
Sleeping birds
The South is sleeping

Thundering blasts
Lightening tanks
Peeling June's asphalt under their
          tread

Anarchy! Fleeing Southern armies
Fleeing Government
The South awakes in terror

The West will not lose South Korea,
The first defense line of
The Asian Cold War

Pelting downpour of great bombs
From the Northern sky
Precise missiles from the Seventh
          Fleet

Marines secretly land at Inchon
Trapping the red army in the South
Oh red brothers

With no road to the North
Your home in ruins already
Where should you go? Lay down
          your arms

Throw away your doomed
          military clothes
It is not Our War anyway
Here are civilian clothes. Put them
          on

Go back to being Asian again –
A single mercy, shared
        brotherhood –
You will survive you will
The Kremlin will not lose North
        Korea,
The first defense line of
The Asian Cold War

Chinese red armies
Cross the Yalu River
Endless Human Waves

Billowing swelling higher
Press down
Recross the 38th

MacArthur withdraws his troops in
        disorder
Who said that by Christmas
The War would be over and that

We UN troops could go home?
Can we go home we prisoners?
Christmas Prison War… are they
        not

The Trinity of this century?
God help us on alien soil
Why should we perish in a Wrong
        War?

The West launches its magic force
        again
"Stop here stop! Who can desecrate
        the 38th?"
Louder louder in grassy eternity

The grasshoppers sing, and sing
      "Withdraw withdraw
Open terrors, secret terrors on
      both sides
Do not move. Listen to the
TALK OF CEASE FIRE

"To be a Penitent Listener is to be
      Holy
You have seen the New Map of Our
      Peninsula:
Between clashing advances and

"Deadly retreats of both forces
The air turns into fire
The earth melts away

"Animals lose their mountains
Humans lose their sun's way – grain's
      way
Stars lose our garden nights, village
      nights

"Parents disappear
Children disappear
Where are our fellow folks?

"In the air, blasted into the air
Fallen on the street, in the ditch
In the water, fallen everywhere

"The years of the Hermit Kingdom
The past fifty centuries are in flames
The road to pristine jewels and relics

The road to Confucian shrines
Buddha's temples and Pagodas
Thatched houses, family trees

Folk songs, spinning hat-ribbons
At peasantry festivals
Flaring native clothes of colorful
         rainbow —

The world's treasure!
How ignorant is the Powers'
War against Pristine Earth, Her
         culture

War against trees, rocks, rivers,
         animals
War against day and night, four
         seasons
War against universal history

Ancient Korea is torn asunder
From the BRIDGE OF NO
         RETURN
One goes South, one goes North"

The grasshoppers collapse into sobbing
Their song stops.
Who can heal our Wounds?

With guns, tanks, missiles
As surgical instruments
What operation will work...

Who can destroy the damned
Demarcation, the 38th?
When can I see my sisters?
         Tell me Yalta tell me

Autumn Love

With the acorn-buried house blown up by the War
With those who could not return to me
I meet Autumn again – my only friend when
All have gone and no one remains here with me

The sunset
Sweet gums and oak leaves
Illuminate an evening in pensive purple
Filled with passion for a candle and indoors

Does the evening know winter is coming?
        What genius
        Creative pensive beauty
        Out of green leaves?

Is he one of us, historical orphans of sorrow
Fated to live outdoors?
        His creation of Autumn love
        Began with the loss of his homeland,

        In his hour of plodding alone
        On the sunset road

Road accept us orphans
Autumn accept us

Defense

Agonized melody, the minor key of
Tchaikovsky dies in a fiery sigh.
In what tone of desolation a soul must die!
It may perish when art leaves.

A troubled soul listens to the end –
            Alone, sundered from events and history,
            The key's search for a tune of
            Soft talk by the evening lamp,

            A desiccating tune in the fiery sigh
            That endeavors to keep his small room
            And to live in beauty and inspiration,

            Pain and daily needs, iron days, violence,
            The mega trend of empty culture...
            Beyond all things Art's gentle defense of
            The goodness of the soul.

Beauty and inspiration never die,
The melody lives. It flows into
The troubled soul standing on the attic ledge,
And guides its shadow gently back into the room
Where a candle flares, and the violin resounds.

Your Image

A young death a terrible world inflicted on you.
You wanted a little mercy for being there on your
Native soil, loving the sun, walking along the
Familiar path with friends and animals.

Your figure – a fragrance of Asian trees, as pure as
Asian peace and water. This is the soil trod by the
First man on earth, our ancestor. Then why need mercy?

Ask whom? Doubts, questions must be swallowed.
The answer has been tested, terrible contested
And re-defined at last by rejecting history.

Life without history? Without calendar years? Yes yes,
There have been no wars no holocausts no pedigree no love
No memory in Asia. What month is it? What century is it?

Somewhere on the familiar path, the emergence of leaves
Reminds us of the seasons with their fairies and legends.

The air is sweet
The lilac sleeps
The lilac dreams

No, you didn't die, you never forget spring,
Your image returns here wanting to live again.

Retrieve

Autumn leaves, winds, family.
Far off a thunderstorm rumbles,
It is the season to go home and stay indoors.

Dried herb strings, the saucepan, the teapot are still
There. God has been in the warm kitchen for centuries.
Mother stirs mushroom soup by the fireside,
The evening candle waits for you to read and write.

Do you have a home, a miracle on the Autumn night?
Home is vulnerable. It is Plundered, destroyed.

The home of the homeless is a candle house of love.
There in the window, the surviving candle, surviving
War and death, evokes a hidden figure in stormy tears.

I can see my mother again in the window,
I can almost touch the warm teapot.

You hear the thunder. I will rekindle the candle
Whenever the storms blow out the flame.
One must know how to live with the wind.

Distant Spring

Spring night
Stars behind the woods
Tiny lilac lanterns along the path.

Granted by a dream
The lilac petals I touch
And mix them with the stars

Believing that
The night is mine
You are with me.

But how hard to believe in solitude
When love is possible here
On this lilac path.

Spring is no one's dream
In the age of carnage,
Of exile and the homeless.

You are not here
Distant Spring, you are,
The shredded one.

Holidays

Lights crown Christmas, wine and snow brew holidays.
In the tavern, on a snowy bench, people dream of
Happiness. A happiness without love, without Spring!
I sense their feelings and toast our wishes.

I seek stars, nights. Winds tear black trees
The surviving tree from long ago when it was fated
To be the Cross-wood over His weakening shoulders.

>   The Cross no one could carry. Flesh is frail,
>   Agony riots. The creation of His love was born
>   In the agony of parting from His flesh.

>   His creation, envisioned in a wilderness
>   Of flowers and in the School of Nature,
>   Needed no philosophy or institution.

>   Through His origin and
>   Roman violence, it was
>   to surmount their atrocity
>   And revere the universe.

To what fresh persuasion should we belong?
I follow Gethsemane stars, Calvary trees.

Brotherhood

Lonely civilization, atonal world,
All is distance.

On the rainy street a melody soaks into
Passers-by, each alone, with a barely useable heart.

"Rainy blues," sad flotsam from the past, you sing.
You, a dark faced Orpheus from the old south.

"Blues" are not only songs, but the timbre of
Broken hearts that seek native souls,
An intimacy of brotherhood.

How many nights have you slept on the roadside?
Your mission is to eliminate cruel distance
By entwining it with people and forgotten lyrics.

Wet leaves turn to ice, tired people
Seek sleep on the open corner.
With loose coins you have earned, you buy food,
Pass it gently to them.
You stand like a candle,
On the street of pain.

Autumn Lamp

A hazy farewell gesture in changing leaves.
To the migrating one, life is unbearable partings.

How far can this unwilling step go?
The mind is split, the home cannot bear your absence.
The crisis of leaving one's home... why? why?
Questions, answers, disasters are the same.

You are not allowed to return or go farther.
Can you cry? Falling leaves touch you,
The twilight flowers welcome you on the roadside.

An opaline lamp glows at the oak tree, as if wishing
To hold your hand and take you into its bower.

The evening air, the lamp, the oak – what a sweet
Enclosure they make a night of migration!

Within it you can hear the cricket,
By the slumbering lamp you can dream over a book.
How I wish to stay here in this safe enclosure
And write an Autumn story.

Wherever you go,
The earth holds and loves you.
You, an apostle of seasons.

Winter Night

The winter night, it is cold and rainy.
No one is on the street.
I'm alone in my room,
free to do whatever I want.
But I can't read or write any more.
This despair takes me to a glass of wine.
I feel guilty to my life
for doing nothing productive.
Tonight is Christmas Eve.
Christ is coming to comfort
And forgive.

January 2011

Epilogue

Now that I have finally come to this point, economic storms have hit hard on us. Everyone is in a rush. A rush to where? To the door? The door is closed. No money for food and rent. Jobs have gone. Stores are vanishing. God grant us food and a bed.

How frail is the human shield against the abyss! In this troubled time my husband of fifty years passed away. Strange that his death occurred around Ash Wednesday of 2009. In his last moments, he wanted to breathe. Is there any way to transform my breath to him? With this senseless question I knocked at the door of nothingness.

I fell on him when he collapsed. No more meaning. No desires. Life does not belong to me anymore.

How insignificant is the writing of this epilogue! I need a little light in this darkness. Agony and suffering escalate inside me. Solitude compounds the suffering, but poetry intervenes like a tender sister, helping me endure the loneliness.

There is not enough love among men to prevent atrocities, wars, massacres, and executions. But love and compassion are the only possibility for survival.

Poetry may take us where our old friends are, or where the setting sun blends with our memories.

I would be glad if my poems could bring warmth or hope to any who are in privation and isolation.

CPSIA information can be obtained at www.ICGtesting.com
Printed in the USA
LVOW070112200312

273878LV00005B/12/P